For Bee

Author David Starling
First Published in 2011
Published by Essex Women's Advisory Group
Copyright © Essex Women's Advisory Group (EWAG) 2011
Printed in England by Juniper House of Print
Harwich Road, Lawford, Manningtree, Essex CO11 2LS

ISBN 978-0-9567397-1-1

Front Cover:
Bawleys and Smacks
painted by Roger Fisher RSMA

Back cover:
Ida built in 1867 and **Charlotte Ellen** built in 1897, both at Brightlingsea. Colne Smack Race 1981
painted by Roger Fisher RSMA

Essex has the longest coastline of any English county. From the Thames in the south to the Stour in the north is about 50 miles; but follow the tidal shore-line of the creeks, islands and estuaries and you will cover nearer 400 miles. On this journey over the centuries you would have met fishermen, bargemen, smugglers, boat-builders, wildfowlers and the captains and crews of the great yachts. You would also have met their grandmothers, mothers, wives, daughters and granddaughters, most as tough as their men - sometimes more so, because it was they who had to hold the family together through hardships and adversity. You would then have begun to understand why so many of these men named their vessels for their women.

Nice-Looking (Essex) Girls Afloat

*M*ehalah. *A regular Essex marshland name. I hope I shall remember it. But I have to carry so many names of nice-looking girls in my head, and of ships I have built, that they run one another down, and I cannot be sure to recall them.*

Mehalah, 1880

The Reverend Sabine Baring-Gould

Blackwater Gals

photo by Den Phillips

Joy

In her recently published autobiography the little Mersea winklebrig **Joy** writes "one of the many pleasures of being a pretty little wooden boat is the friendly waves and salutes you receive wherever you go". She was built just after the second World War by Alf Last at Maldon as the barge boat for the Thames Barge **Joy** in the same yard as the barge herself had been built in the first year of the first World War.

In 1971 she became a film star as the little sailing boat in the TV film of Paul Gallico's *The Snow Goose*. Richard Harris played Rhayader, the artist with the dark beard, claw hand and bent spine, who lived alone in the abandoned lighthouse in the Great Marsh on the Essex Coast. Jenny Agutter played Fritha, "no more than twelve, slender, dirty, nervous and timid as a bird, but beneath the grime as eerily beautiful as a marsh faery," who brought the snow goose, wounded by the wildfowlers, to Philip Rhayader.

Fritha

But the real star of the film is **Joy** which Philip sails to Dunkirk and brings off boat-load after boat-load of soldiers to the bigger ships lying off-shore, with the snow goose circling above the shrapnel.

It is a love story of such beauty and pathos and ends with Philip being machine-gunned by the Stukas, the snow goose "dropping out of a crimsoned eastern sky to circle the lighthouse in a last farewell" and Fritha, "from the ancient powers of the blood that was in her, knowing that Rhayader would not return…………."

"…….would not return, did not return," has been a recurring theme over the centuries for those Essex men and their families for whom the sea has been not just their living but their way of life; building and sailing the barges, oyster smacks and great yachts of the nineteenth and early twentieth centuries. It is no wonder that the smackmen, who braved the winter gales to fish the North Sea, would also turn out in the great gale and snow storm of December 1875 to go to the aid of the **Deutschland** aground on the Kentish Knock.

....

Into the snow she sweeps,
Hurling the haven behind,
The Deutschland, on Sunday; and so the sky keeps,
For the infinite air is unkind,
And the sea flint-flake, black-backed in the regular blow,
Sitting Eastnortheast, in cursed quarter, the wind;
Wiry and white-fiery and whirlwind-swivellèd snow
Spins to the widow-making unchilding unfathering deeps.

She drove in the dark to leeward,
She struck - not a reef or a rock
But the combs of a smother of sand: night drew her
Dead to the Kentish Knock;
And she beat the bank down with her bows and the ride of her keel:
The breakers rolled on her beam with ruinous shock;
And canvas and compass, the whorl and the wheel
Idle for ever to waft her or wind her with, these she endured.

....

The Wreck of the Deutschland   Gerard Manley Hopkins

All Saints Church Brightlingsea   *photo by the author*

All Saints Church Brightlingsea records, in the tiles around the church, all those Brightlingsea men who have lost their lives at sea since 1872. This was the year of the induction as vicar of the Reverend Arthur Pertwee, whose idea it was to record the deaths on tiles.

The great gale of March 1883 took the lives of nineteen Brightlingsea men from three smacks (out of a Brightlingsea fleet of fifteen) which foundered without trace off the Terschelling Banks. Thirty-two children were left fatherless. But none of the three smacks had women's names.

3

Oyster Girl

Hervey Benham's book *Down Tops'l, the Story of the East Coast Sailing-Barges,* lists some six hundred barges, of which about a quarter had women's Christian names. Were they named for wives, mothers, daughters, or because the builder or owner just liked the name? Or were daughters sometimes named after boats? The tiles record the loss of 212 lives between 1872 and 1980, but only fifteen of these were from vessels with women's names. Amongst the most poignant are "Albert Edward Layzell, aged 25, lost from wreck of Barge **Ada** of Harwich off Portland. December 22, 1888"; "Albert Rouse, aged 26, drowned from the Smack **Sibyl** off Emsworth. May 8, 1890"; "Alfred King, aged 15, drowned from the Barge **Little Suzannah** in Queenborough Swale. October 17, 1892", and from the evocatively named smack, the **Oyster Girl**, "Albert Bines aged 32, lost in the North Sea. December, 1895".

Do these statistics mean that vessels, female as we know all vessels to be, when blessed with feminine names are thereby doubly blessed and the safer for it? Who knows?

A search through the Register Books, which list all the owners of all British merchant vessels, shows that often a former owner's widow would be listed as the owner by inheritance of a boat with the same name as herself.

This, which applied more to small vessels, such as smacks, which had a sole owner, than to larger vessels such as barges, which tended to have several owners, could well have been a very good reason for an owner naming his boat for his wife. The square stern smack **Margaret** was built at Rowhedge in 1853 for Elijah Bowles, and, when he died in 1871, she passed to his widow, Margaret Bowles. Likewise the **Mary Ann**, another square stern smack, built for Daniel Harvey of East Donyland in 1861, passed to his widow, Mary Ann Harvey when he died in 1873. And, an exception to prove the rule: the spritsail barge **John and Ann** built at Brightlingsea in 1865 and in the sole ownership of John Knight passed, when he died in 1872, to his widow, Ann Knight.

The Barge **Joy** herself had a miraculous escape when a "terrible blow came out of a clear sky one day just after Christmas in 1914, stripping roofs off the houses in Paglesham village and causing much loss of life on the water". Eleven bargemen were lost that night. The **Joy** was among the fleet of barges, "only half loaded, which probably saved her, for she dragged over the Ridge onto the Mouse, and when her crew looked out in the morning, they could see seven barges sunk round them…." *Hervey Benham, Down Tops'l*

Charlotte

But it wasn't just fearless seamanship and instinctive understanding of the shoals and sandbanks that served to keep safe water under the keels of the smacks and barges. Trinity House, incorporated by Royal Charter in 1514, was charged by Henry VIII to regulate the pilotage of ships in the King's streams and, in 1566, the Seamarks Act gave them powers to set up "So many beacons, marks and signs for the sea, whereby the dangers may be avoided and escaped and ships the better come into their ports without peril." The other great peril was that vessels at night showed only a single white light and there were no rules of the road. The Wivenhoe smack, the **Charlotte**, lost off the Norfolk coast in 1836, steered for what her skipper thought was the Dudgeon light, only to find as she was smashed to pieces by the paddles of the steamer **Perth**, that it was her single white lantern **Charlotte** had been steering on. It was soon after that Trinity House brought in rules for side lights and rights of way.

Patricia and Galatea

Trinity House, based in Harwich, fulfils its appointed task to this day, and the two Trinity House Vessels, THV **Patricia** and THV **Galatea** must be up with the winners in the list of Nice-Looking Girls Afloat. The first **Patricia** was converted from the SY **Miranda** in 1920 and named for Patricia Ramsay (Princess Patricia of Connaught), daughter of HRH Prince Arthur Duke of Connaught, who was Master of Trinity House from 1910 to 1942. Today's **Patricia**, launched in 1982, is the third THV to bear that name.

THV **Patricia**   *photo Trinity House*

THV **Galatea**, launched in 2007, was named for THV **Galatea** (1868), herself named for the then-Master (1866 - 1893), HRH Prince Alfred Duke of Edinburgh's first Royal Naval command. The first HMS **Galatea** was a 20-gun sixth-rate launched in 1776 and broken up in 1783 and the last, the eighth, was a Leander Class Frigate launched in 1963.

All twenty-six Leander Class Frigates had names taken from classical mythology. **Galatea** herself first appeared in Ovid's *Metamorphoses* as one of the Nereides, fifty goddess-nymphs of the sea. Her name means either "the goddess of calm seas" from galēnē and theia or "milky-

white" from galaktos.

Out of the 32 ships in Nelson's fleet at Trafalgar, 16 had names from mythology; but amongst the hundreds and hundreds of Essex smacks and barges hardly one; and the reason is quite clear: our politicians of the 18thC had learnt the classics at school and probably not much else. The Earl of Sandwich, who was First Lord of the Admiralty from 1771 to 1782, in particular, was said to have kept a copy of Lemprière's classical dictionary on his desk and simply picked a name from it. The Northseamen had learned other, perhaps more practical, things.

HMS **Galatea**   *photo Navy Photos*

Britannia

Throughout the Golden Age of Sail, the finest sailing and steam yachts were captained and crewed from the Essex villages and spent their winters laid up in the mud berths of Brightlingsea, Wivenhoe, Rowhedge and Tollesbury. The most famous and successful of these was undoubtedly **Britannia**, King George V's beloved GL Watson designed 100 foot racing cutter. Britannia, the name the Romans gave the country they began to conquer in AD43, was personified by them as a goddess, armed with a spear and shield and wearing a centurion's helmet. In 1923, already thirty years old, **Britannia** was converted from gaff to Bermudan rig and came under the command of Captain Albert Turner of Wivenhoe for unbelievable successes

The King's racing flag

racing against the new Big Class yachts, the Js, until the King's death in 1936.

One of those Js, **Velsheda**, built in 1933 in Gosport and crewed from the south coast, was named for her owner's three daughters, Velma, Sheila and Daphne. Neither this, nor the week spent each year racing in the Big Class off Southend, qualifies her as an Essex Girl; but it's a good story about a clearly diplomatic father!

The mastheadsman in **Britannia** was the skipper's nephew, Johnny Turner, who sailed aloft, 150 feet above the deck, for the last ten years of **Britannia's** life, and his brother, Fred, was the boatman. But the best remembered of Captain Turner's nephews was Ernie, who never, in fact, sailed in the **Britannia**.

Britannia in her 1893 rig

photo Mersea Museum John Leather Collection

Xanthe

Ernie Turner, who died in 1978, turned in his retirement in Wivenhoe to painting. Much in the same naïve style as Alfred Wallis, who, at the age of 70 in 1920, took to painting in his native Cornwall, they both recorded on cardboard, hardboard, driftwood, seldom canvas, the vessels and scenes of their life on the waterfront and at sea. One of Ernie's finest paintings is of the Rowhedge smack **Xanthe** sailing up river past Wivenhoe - a smack with a name from Greek mythology. **Xanthe** was one of the Oceanids, the 3,000 daughters of the Titans Oceanus and Tethys. One of her sisters was Amphitrite, the consort of the god Poseidon.

Xanthe *painted by Ernie Turner*   *collection James Dodds*

The smack **Xanthe** was always spoken of in Rowhedge as the X-anthe, hence the caption on Ernie Turner's painting "Exanthe". She was owned by Captain Bill Cranfield, who spent the winter stowboating, while another **Xanthe** was laid up in a mud berth in Rowhedge. Captain Cranfield was the professional skipper of this other **Xanthe**, a 60 foot cutter designed and built in 1890 at Rowhedge for a High Court Judge, Sir Arthur Channell. And there was also **Xantha**, a 138 ton yawl, built by Thomas Harvey in Wivenhoe in 1865 for Lord Alfred Paget, fifth son of the Marquess of Anglesey, and the most prolific yacht owner of the nineteenth century. During his life he owned over forty yachts, and the **Xantha** (later renamed **Gertrude**) was said to be the best racer he ever owned.

Lord Alfred's father, who lost a leg at Waterloo, was, of course, the owner of the renowned **Pearl**.

Xanthe CK103
photo Mersea Museum John Leather Collection

Pearl

The cutter yacht **Pearl** was built in 1820 by Philip John Sainty, a larger than life character - shipowner and master, shipbuilder and smuggler, with a reputation for building fast cutters - who, at one time or another, built ships at all the Colneside locations. When he died in 1844, aged 90, he had had three wives, at least eighteen children, had been bankrupt twice and had been imprisoned for smuggling. The trouble was that he was in Chelmsford Gaol when Lord Anglesey wanted him to build his yacht, having been caught smuggling gold sovereigns to Holland in a double-skinned smack that he had built for the job. The Marquess is reputed to have said that "even if he were in hell he would have him out". Lord Anglesey obtained a pardon from the Prince Regent; the probable reality being that he paid some huge fines.

Clinker-built below the wales and carvel above, 92 feet from her stern to the end of her bowsprit and measuring 127.5 tons, the **Pearl** was a giant amongst the yachts of her time. In an era of straight stems and bluff bows, she had a fine entry, a long run and a delicately proportioned counter. She was fast; but it was soon realised that she was winning because of her length and tonnage (hull speed being a function of wetted length) and not just her fine lines, and a number of large yachts were built on the south coast to compete with the "Essex Flier". Notwithstanding Sainty's reputation for building fast cutters, be they yachts, smacks, for the revenue service or smuggling, in 1826 the Cowes-built 100 ton revenue cutter **Vigilant** challenged the **Pearl** and two other yachts to a race round the Needles and back to Cowes. The Vigilant won by such a big margin that "her cheering crew sailed her back to circle the yachts before they finished."

Camper & Nicholson, founded in 1782, rebuilt the Pearl in their Gosport yard as a yawl in 1873. She was the oldest yacht afloat when she was broken up in 1902; but for length of service she was no match for a 30 foot oyster smack, built in 1808 by Williamsons at Maldon and still sailing strongly today...

Pearl with single reef in mainsail and squaresail yard stowed

National Maritime Museum

Boadicea

Boadicea   *photo by Simon Gregor*

At the time of the Roman conquest of southern Britain Queen Boadicea ruled the Iceni tribe of East Anglia alongside her husband King Prasutagus. Cassius Dio described this magnificent woman as "...very tall, the glance of her eye most fierce, her voice harsh. A great mass of the reddest hair fell down to her hips. Her appearance was terrifying".

After Prasutagus' death, his lands and household were plundered by order of the Governor, Suetonius Paulinus. Not content with taking all the property and lands, Suetonius had Prasutagus' widow Boadicea publicly flogged and her daughters raped by Roman slaves. Not surprisingly these outrages provoked the Iceni and other tribes to rebel against the Romans. The Britons at first had great successes and captured the hated Roman settlement of Camulodunum (Colchester) and the Roman division there was routed.

Boadicea and her allies gave no quarter in their victories and when Londinium and Verulamium (St. Albans) were stormed, the defenders fled and the towns were sacked and burned. The revolting Britons even desecrated the Roman cemeteries, mutilating statues and breaking tombstones. Some of these mutilated statues can be seen today in Colchester Museum.

But finally Suetonius decided to challenge Boadicea and assembled an army of 10,000. The historian Tacitus in his *Annals of Rome* gives a very vivid account of the final battle, which was fought in the Midlands in AD61.

Boadicea and her daughters drove round in her chariot to all the tribes before the battle, exhorting them to be brave. She cried that she

Boadicea   *photo by Simon Gregor*

was descended from mighty men but she was fighting as an ordinary person for her lost freedom, her bruised body and outraged daughters. To her army she cried:

"Win the battle or perish: that is what I, a woman, will do; you men can live on in slavery if that's what you want."

The Britons attacked. But…… Tacitus records that 80,000 Britons were killed. The Roman losses amounted to 400 dead, with a slightly larger number wounded. Boadicea was not killed in the battle but took poison rather than be taken alive by the Romans.

The Warrior Queen who fought the might of Rome is remembered by the bronze statue of her riding high in her chariot, designed by Thomas Thorneycroft, on the Thames embankment next to the Houses of Parliament. Norfolk rather than Essex Girl she may have been; but Essex now counts her as one of their finest.

She is also remembered by her namesake, probably the oldest sailing vessel in Europe that is still in regular use. **Boadicea** was built in 1808 as an oyster smack and was worked commercially until 1938. Since then she has been owned by the same family, working the boat for pleasure under sail, pulling a trawl or oyster dredges in order to keep the old skills alive. During the spring and summer **Boadicea** can be found regularly racing against other smacks and classic yachts and in a stiff breeze she very much holds her own. During the autumn she still drift-nets for herring.

Boadicea CK 213, built 1808   *photo by Den Phillips*

Sallie and Hyacinth

Hyacinth, sailed by Millie and Alice - clear winners in the Nice Looking Girls Afloat Stakes   *photo by Den Phillips*

Hyacinth, Heybridge Basin Regatta 2007   *photo by Den Phillips*

The smack **Hyacinth** CK 256, built in 1900 by Aldous, was named after the flower, not the girl. And there is a real life **Fritha**; but sadly not in Essex. The fictional Fritha, who starred with **Joy** in The Snow Goose, has given her name to a 74 foot Murray Peterson designed brigantine sailing out of Fairhaven, Massachusetts.

Sallie CK224 Shotley 1993   *photo by the author*

Ida built 1867 **Charlotte Ellen** built 1897 - both at Brightlingsea. Colne Smack Race 1981
painted by Roger Fisher RSMA

The smack **Sallie** CK 224 was also built at Aldous's yard in Brightlingsea in 1907. We do not know for whom she was named; but in 1964 she was owned by Peter and Janet Light, who gave birth to a baby girl and named her for their beloved smack, **Sallie**. Human Sallie can now usually be found in Antigua doing important things like applying gold leaf to the cove lines of classic yachts. Had Sallie been born a year later, she might well have been less lucky, for by that time her parents owned a Baltic trader called **Solvig**. Solveig in Peer Gynt and Solvig, girls' names in Scandinavia, both mean worshipper of the sun. Equally she might have been christened Joy, for Janet also owned the little winklebrig **Joy**, which we met at the beginning of this essay. And Sallie's twelve year old daughter is called Mehalah.

Ida CK3 Colne Smack Race 1981 *photo by the author*

Helen & Violet

Helen & Violet LO262 and **Doris** LO284 before the Colne Smack Race 1982   *painted by Roger Fisher RSMA*

In about 1890 John and Herbert Cann took over the yard in Harwich which their father George, originally from Brightlingsea, had established in 1868. They built mainly barges and barge boats; but about twelve bawleys were built. John Cann designed very shapely vessels and **Helen & Violet** (1906) and **Doris** (1909) were the fastest of the type. **Helen & Violet** was built for James Kimber of Leigh who, it is believed, named her for his two daughters. She fished out of Leigh until the mid thirties when she was sold and worked out of Brightlingsea for another thirty-five years. Since 1972 she has been in private hands; but has remained in Colne.

Jim Spencer at the helm of **Helen & Violet**
photo Caroline Spencer

This iconic picture of the late Jim Spencer, boatbuilder, sailor and truest of men, has been enshrined in Brightlingsea history by the heraldic artist and calligrapher David Truzzi-Franconi using it for the sign of the waterside pub.

13

Maria

Maria CK21 in the Blackwater 2008

The Harris family were boat builders in Rowhedge from the early years of the nineteenth century. Peter Harris took over the yard in about 1860 and during the next 38 years built 54 yachts and more than 40 smacks. His first two vessels were large first class smacks (the 50 ft **Secret** and the 53 ft **Pioneer**, both launched in 1864; the latter, beautifully restored, can be seen sailing out of Brightlingsea). In 1866 the **Maria** was built for a Mr John Gunn of Wivenhoe. She, too, was a first class smack of 48ft length on deck and 67ft to the tip of her bowsprit. Sunk for eleven years after WW2, after collision with a trawler, she is now sailing again, also out of Brightlingsea, after a four year restoration completed in 2008 at the St Osyth Boatyard; a restoration which won

her the Classic Boat Magazine "Restoration of the Year Award" against competition from some very fancy yachts.

The winter fishing for these big smacks was largely for oysters; across to the Terschelling Banks (112 miles to the east of Orfordness), the French coast and down channel to Jersey, the Cornish coast and round to Swansea and one year to the Firth of Forth. Often, if not always, it was to the fury of, and attack by, the local fishermen. Even now a CK registered vessel does not find a particularly warm welcome in St Helier harbour!

But they also fished for sprats: the Stowboaters. "The stowboat net and its gear were unique in elaborate complexity. They parallel the rig of the spritsail sailing barge, perhaps because both were designed, or evolved, to perform the impossible - the sailing barge to enable two men to take 150 tons of cargo up a farmer's creek or across the North Sea, the stowboater to set a marine trap capable of snaring ten tons of fish without mechanical aid." *Hervey Benham, The Stowboaters.*

This photograph shows **Maria** rigged for stowboating in shallow water. The upper baulk is hauled up clear of the water, snug under the bowsprit, and the lower baulk is ready for lowering to the bottom.

Maria rigged for stowboating

photo Paul Winter

Brightlingsea handled half the east coast sprat landings. Some were pickled in barrels with salt, bay leaves and spices, often for export to Europe and Russia, and some were smoked or cured. But a good catch of prime fish landed too late could find a market glutted and the price of a bushel fallen from a few shillings to a few pence - probably just for manure. It was a hard, very hard, way of earning a living. There is no doubt that, soaked and frozen in a snow-swept February gale, many a crew member's thoughts would have been on the forthcoming summer's racing in the big yachts and the steady money that this would provide.

Stowboat gear - *model by Hervey Benham*
Mersea Museum

15

Mehalah

Gallico's Fritha was in many ways the soul sister of Baring-Gould's even more tragic Mehalah, known in the marshes as Glory, who lived in the West Mersea salt marshes at the beginning of the nineteenth century and "might have been taken for a sailor boy but for the profusion of her black hair…. She wore a blue knitted Guernsey and across the breast woven in red wool was the name of the vessel, Gloriana. **Mehalah** was tall, lithe and firm as a young pine. ….the evening sun lit her brown gipsy face, burnt in her large eyes, and made coppery lights in her dark hair".

The Reverend Sabine Baring-Gould (1834-1924) was a Devonian, who, in 1871 became the rector for ten years of East Mersea. A hagiographer, antiquarian, novelist and eclectic scholar, he wrote many books, including novels and compilations of folk songs; in all more than 1,240 publications. He is remembered particularly as a writer of hymns, the best-known being "Onward, Christian Soldiers". But such militarism and triumphalism are not, apparently, appropriate in the modern church and it has now in some places become "Onward, Christian Pilgrims"; but fortunately still sung to Sir Arthur Sullivan's marvellous tune.

The Reverend Sabine Baring-Gould

...the evening sun lit

her brown gipsy face,

burnt in her large eyes,

and made coppery lights

in her dark hair...

It was while acting as a curate that he met and fell in love with the 16-year-old daughter of a mill hand. He sent her to live with a vicar's family for two years for an education on manners before marrying her. Their marriage lasted until her death 48 years later. When he buried his wife in 1916 he had carved on her tombstone Dimidium Animae Meae ("Half my Soul").

Despite her beauty and the utter magic of her tragic tale, there appear to be very few vessels named for **Mehalah**. Certainly there was a 3 ton centre-board sloop built in Maldon in 1888, a 14 tonner built in Lymington in 1947 and a 47 foot Sparkman and Stephens cutter built in the Far East in the 1980s. She was built for an American dentist and was, very appropriately, named Sweet Tooth. But her new English owner, a Younger Brother of Trinity House, changed her name to **Mehalah** to remind him of his beloved Essex, and sailed her home via Nova Scotia, the Baltic, Corsica and Croatia (not exactly a great-circle course!).

And this brings us back to Trinity House and the **Ready**.

Ready (Mirosa)

The Thames Barge **Ready** was built in 1892 by John Howard in Maldon and was used primarily for carrying hay, straw and timber between the port of London and rivers along the Kentish, Essex and Suffolk coasts.

In the 1930s she passed into the ownership of Francis & Gilders of Colchester who, in 1947, sold her original

Mirosa

photo by Den Phillips

name to Trinity House for a new lightship tender and therefore needed a new name for their barge. Joshua Francis's daughter was called Rosa; but the story goes that it was her master, Billy "Bundock" Austin, who countered the proposal that she be called My Rosa with **Mirosa.**

Mirosa

photo by Den Phillips

She continued trading under sail until 1955 when she was sold to become a timber lighter back in her native Maldon. However ten years later she was re-rigged for sailing. Based in Faversham, in immaculate condition, she and the **Edme** (built by Canns of Harwich in 1898 and named after the EDME Company - English Diastatic Malt Extract - situated at Mistley Quay) are the last two Thames Barges to be earning their living, chartering, still without an engine.

Victoria and **Ready** in Basin Reach Winter 1947

*Maurice Findlay - mate of the **Ready***

photos Mersea Museum - Frank Thompson Collection

Hebe

"............we shall fight on the beaches, we shall fight on the landing grounds, we shall fight in the fields and in the streets, we shall fight in the hills; we shall never surrender............"

Churchill after Dunkirk

From 27th May to 4th June 1940, a staggering total of 338,266 British and Allied soldiers were rescued.

Operation Dynamo, as the evacuation was known and named for its headquarters in the underground dynamo room under Dover Castle, was under the overall command of Vice Admiral Bertram Ramsay, a former pupil of Colchester Royal Grammar School, who was knighted for his success in the endeavour.

Rear Admiral William Wake-Walker, who was in actual command of the shipping off Dunkirk, recorded the moment he saw the flotilla of around 700 little ships arriving: "I saw for the first time that strange procession of craft of all kinds that has become famous. Tugs towing dinghies, lifeboats and all manner of pulling boats, small motor yachts, motor launches, drifters, Dutch scoots, Thames barges, fishing boats and pleasure steamers, all arriving in the nick of time to rescue Britain's surrounded army."

The Admiral reached Dunkirk on the minesweeper HMS **Hebe** early on 30th May, and for the rest of the evacuation spent most of his time directing operations from small boats under constant fire. The following day he transferred to the destroyer, HMS **Keith**; but within 24 hours she had been disabled and the Admiral transferred his flag (a naval figure of speech as there was, in fact, no flag to transfer, but one was created out of an Admiralty issue dishcloth and a pot of red

Barbara Jean and **Ena** Ipswich Dock 1930s
Hervey Benham, Down Tops'l
photo Mersea Museum - John Leather Collection

paint) to HM **MTB102**. He had intended to transfer to another destroyer, HMS **Boadicea**; but she too had been disabled and sunk by air attacks. **MTB102** was Vosper's 68ft Prototype Motor Torpedo Boat and the fastest vessel in the Royal Navy in WW2. Maintained by the **MTB102** Trust, she is still afloat and in operation (visit **www.mtb102.com**).

Sixteen Thames Barges in all were part of the heroic fleet. Ten were sunk; seven with girls' names, R. & W. Paul's **Barbara Jean** and **Aidie**, the only Essex vessels, both built in Brightlingsea in 1924 and named after the daughters of Russell Paul, and **Duchess, Doris, Ethel Everard, Lady Rosebery and Valonia.**

Six of the sixteen were owned by R. & W. Paul of Ipswich, including **Ena**, built in the Navy Yard at Harwich in 1906 and owned by Paul's ever since. **Ena's** part in the evacuation is the stuff of legend.

The Association of Dunkirk Little Ships reports it like this (visit **www.adls.org.uk** for hours of interesting browsing):

"During their crossing they endured constant air attacks. Finally Alfred Page, her skipper, was ordered to beach her close to the smaller sand barge **H.A.C.** As the Germans closed in, the crews of both barges were ordered to abandon their ships and escape on a minesweeper to England.

"There are two eye-witness accounts of what happened next. Alex Smith recalls how he, with 30 men of the Duke of Wellington's Regiment commanded by Captain David Strangeways their Adjutant, arrived on La Panne beach. They could not believe their luck when they saw two barges in seaworthy condition anchored and almost afloat. They took possession of the barge **H.A.C.** while Colonel McKay with his men of the 19th Field Regiment, Royal Artillery boarded the **Ena** which was beached not far away. Captain Atley of the East Yorks Regiment, also remembers the event. He was at the mole at Dunkirk and, together with one of his men, made a raft. Using shovels, they rowed out to the **Ena.** They helped 36 other men on board including three wounded and by 0800 they were under sail.

"Then, according to Alex Smith, the two ships got involved in one of the most remarkable barge races of all time. Under constant enemy bombardment and machine-gun fire, they crossed the Channel. Captain Atley recalls that by midnight they took a back-bearing on Dunkirk and found they had gone too far South-West. His only sailing experience had been on the Broads and he had

forgotten to put the leeboards down. So they altered course to North-Northwest and finally sighted the North Goodwin buoy. They then had to tack again towards the South Goodwin lightship. Eventually the **Ena** was picked up by a tug or fleet auxiliary and taken into Margate. Since the harbour was full, the empty barge was then towed out and left anchored off Deal.

"The shipping manager of R & W Paul, who had presumed the **Ena** lost on the beaches of Dunkirk, was amazed when he was told and asked what he proposed to do about it. Alfred Page, her skipper, by then back in Ipswich, was sent to recover her. He found the **Ena** seaworthy but stripped of all her gear. 'They had taken the sweeps, mooring lines, fenders and even my false teeth which I had left behind in a glass of water by my bunk!' he said, 'you can't trust these men of Kent!' So he sailed her back to Ipswich."

In 1974 the **Ena** was transferred to Paul's Social and Sports Club and for a further twenty-five years she competed in sailing barge matches on the Thames, the Medway, Blackwater and Orwell. She was always the easiest of the barges to recognise - from about 1885 all the barges of R & W Paul carried a white cross on the topsail to identify them at a distance at sea or over the banks of a river.

For certain there are children and grandchildren of those who sailed in them to Dunkirk named for both the **Barbara Jean** and the **Ena** - and one suspects many more.

Another of the seven Thames Barges to return was **Beatrice Maud**. Built in 1910 by Whites, at Sittingbourne in Kent, she was laid up as business fell away after WW1. Brought back into trade in the early thirties, her first master was believed to have been Captain Nobby Finch from Mistley, When Captain Finch retired, Captain Lionel Horlock took his position. He was also from Mistley and a member of the well-known Horlock family of bargemen. It was Lionel Horlock who took her to Dunkirk and had to leave her there.

She crossed the channel on 31st May, and like many other barges, was left stranded on the beach. Perhaps her skipper relied on her shallow draft to enable her to re-float on the incoming tide. Or her crew may have been ordered to beach her to enable other vessels to use her as a boarding platform. In the event it proved providential. Some two hundred and sixty soldiers, reported to be French, led by a Lieutenant Heron, a yachtsman, boarded her on 4th June and a British Naval ship towed her in to Dover the following day.

Hebe, in Greek mythology, was the goddess of youth, the daughter of Zeus and Hera. She was cupbearer to the gods until replaced by Ganymede, a prince of Troy and the most attractive of mortals, which led Zeus to abduct him in the form of an eagle. There was nothing new in having a warship named for a heroine from classical mythology; but there was an earlier **Hebe**, a Colchester smack, who, like her later namesake, had a tangled time off the French coast.

The bigger Essex smacks went away in February and March down channel, often as far as the Channel Islands; but their fishing was harassed by the French and in 1832 the whole Colne fleet came home declaring that "no Englishman felt safe for they had no one to protect them". The next year the **Hebe** was seized, allegedly for dredging within the one league (three mile) limit. The smack was detained and the crew set adrift. Meantime the French long-lining luggers continued freely to take shelter in the Colne, whilst the Essex smacks were not permitted to anchor anywhere near the French coast. Plus ça change……!

Ena in Ipswich Dock 1986

photo by R W Smith

Letitia

In St. Clement's Churchyard, Leigh-on-Sea, is a memorial to the heroic fishermen of Leigh who went to rescue the British soldiers trapped on the Dunkirk beaches. Four fishermen were killed and this memorial recognises the bravery and sacrifice of all the fishermen involved with this rescue.

The Leigh cocklers were broad-beamed, flat-bottomed gaff cutters, typically of some 36ft length, designed to be beached at high tide on the sandbanks, while the fishermen got out to collect cockles and shrimps for the London market. They would go cockling from Easter to October and shrimping in the winter. They were therefore ideal for the shallow waters off Dunkirk.

The **Letitia**, built in 1938 by Johnson & Johnson and a mere 30ft. in length, sailed from Leigh, her skipper Arthur Dench, with five other cocklers, **Renown, Reliant, Endeavour, Defender** and **Resolute**. There was no hesitation on the part of the Leigh men: all the fishermen volunteered to take their own boats, and a few more went as crews on other boats. **Letitia's** crew was Arthur Dench, his son Jim Dench and Ken Horner.

The official Operation Dynamo log shows that the flotilla of six cockle boats

The launch of **Letitia** 1938, Arthur Dench on deck with Pip the dog and his son Jim throwing the water.

left Southend after taking on fuel and stores at 12.30 on Friday May 31st, passed Margate Roads and was then ordered directly to Dunkirk.

At 18.20 they came under air attack and had to scatter, narrowly to avoid being bombed - one man said a stick of bombs dropped so close that he could read the yellow lettering on them.

At 19.15 they were at Dunkirk Roads, and found it impractical to work off Dunkirk beach as ordered as the tide was going out and they would be left high and dry.

At 21.30 they embarked troops from the North Mole and transferred them to waiting ships. The swell was then too great to work off the mole and they went further in to the harbour.

By the time it was dark they had made several trips. A destroyer lay sunk across the entrance; oil barrels and debris floated on the oily water and, on one side of the harbour, the steamer **Eagle** lay sinking after a direct hit down her funnel. As they picked their way through the debris to the pier there seemed to be less men waiting, and they were getting choosey: " . . . not going back on that bloody thing" they shouted. Eric Osborne, skipper of **Resolute**, quite understood: "when you are not a cockle fisherman and consider the idea of a 36 foot boat seen from 36 feet above, it doesn't inspire a lot of confidence."

Eric continued that the fishermen decided to go ashore, partly so that they could say that they had been on French soil, and partly to persuade reluctant soldiers to come on board. At that moment they had their narrowest escape when German guns found the range of the dock and sparks and shrapnel flew all over: "We came down that ladder faster than we went

At 18.20 they came under air attack and had to scatter, narrowly to avoid being bombed - one man said a stick of bombs dropped so close that he could read the yellow lettering on them.

up. It only lasted three or four minutes. We had our full load and motored outside the harbour."

At some point **Letitia's** rudder was damaged, and, on her last trip out, she off-loaded her troops on to the steamer **Ben and Lucy** and was taken in tow for the trip home. The flotilla embarked for England at about midnight. They had ferried about 1,000 men, and those still under their own power took about 360 more back with them.

As they travelled back they picked up the cockler **Renown**. Arthur Dench tells the story in his own words:

"We began our journey home. Soon we saw another boat coming behind us. It was the **Renown**. Frankie yelled that they had engine trouble. They made fast to our stern and we towed them, about 3½ fathoms of rope being the distance between us. That was at 1.15 a.m. and, tired out, the engineer, the seaman and the signaller went to 'turn in' as our work seemed nearly done. We were congratulating ourselves when, at about 1.50, a terrible explosion took place. The **Renown** had hit a mine and a hail of splinters came down on our deck. In the pitch dark we could do nothing except pull in the tow rope, which was just as we had passed it to the **Renown** about three quarters of an hour before. But no sign of the **Renown**. These were Leigh men who had lived quiet, respectable lives and never done a bad turn to anyone. Better living boys you could never have wished to meet. They knew nothing of war, they went to save, not to fight. They had done their work and now suddenly on their way home there came annihilation. It was a small tragedy in the great disaster of those days of war, yet great in the hearts of Leigh people. We still wonder why their bravery should have been paid thus."

The boats reported to Ramsgate where they were told that only the very fast boats would be used for the last trips over, so they were discharged. They returned sadly to Leigh-on-Sea where their families were waiting for them on the beach. Florence Dench remembered seeing her father returning covered in black soot and oil from Dunkirk. Of course he then had the very sad duty of telling the families of the lost fishermen what had happened.

Arthur Dench returned to cockling and shrimping in **Letitia** until 1947 when he had **Letitia** III built on similar lines but with a slightly lower free-board. The logic of the names is that his daughter was Letitia I, the boat was **Letitia** II and the new boat was **Letitia** III.

Letitia LO 220   *photo by Michael Feather*

Guide of Dunkirk

On 1st June 1940, RNLB ON826, intended to be the Clacton lifeboat, was still at her builders, Rowhedge Ironworks, and still un-named when she was ordered to take part in the Dunkirk evacuation. Crewed by men from Frinton and Walton she made two trips and, badly damaged by shellfire, she returned to her builders for extensive repairs. Self-righting, with 8 tons displacement and a draft of 2ft 9ins, she was designed for launching from the beach and had been paid for with funds raised by the Girl Guides Association. After Dunkirk she served at Cadgwith Cove, Cornwall and in 1947 was named **Guide of Dunkirk**. She was sold in 1963, when the station closed, and her new private owner changed her name to **Girl Guide**. Nineteen RNLI lifeboats, from Great Yarmouth to Poole, went to Dunkirk.

Edian Courtauld

RNLB **Edian Courtauld** was built at Cowes and, at the beginning of November, 1953, she made the passage to Walton in what at times was a severe southerly gale. She was a 46ft 9in Watson class boat powered by two 40hp Ferry diesel engines, with an amidships steering position and a deck cabin to give shelter to the crew. She was the gift of Augustine Courtauld (always known as August) and named for his mother, Edith Anne (Edian) who had died in 1951.

Edian Courtauld launching on service 21st April 1971

photo courtesy of John Steer

Edian Courtauld naming ceremony 20th July 1954
photo Frinton & Walton Heritage Trust Collection

At a ceremony at the Albion breakwater on 20th July 1954, the new lifeboat was handed over to the Walton and Frinton Branch and named by the Duchess of Kent, President of the RNLI.

The **Edian Courtauld's** last life-saving launch took place on 29th May 1977 when, in strong northerly winds, she took in tow the yacht **Caprice**, which had lost her rudder hitting the Gunfleet. In her 24 years at Walton she had launched 227 times, rescuing 143 lives. Her final, and sadly unsuccessful, launch, before being placed in the relief fleet, was on 9th July 1977 in response to a man overboard from the yacht **Mary Jane**.

During her last annual overhaul she was fitted with a single-use inflatable air bag, designed to right her in the event of a capsize. After two fairly recent disasters, the RNLI had decided to make their entire fleet of off-shore lifeboats self-righting. All new classes such as the Waveney were inherently self-righting; but the older designs were fitted with air bags. The success of this system was proved when lifeboats at Barra Island and Salcombe capsized and were righted, using this method, with no loss of life. *John Steer, Walton & Frinton Lifeboat A Station History 1884-2005.*

August Courtauld died on 3rd March 1959 and, three days later, his coffin was taken on board the lifeboat and buried at sea near the West Rocks.

In 1974 RNLB **Augustine Courtauld**, a Waveney class lifeboat, came into service in Poole, given in August's memory by his brother, Peter (and the Mayor of Poole's Appeal). In her nine years on station she was launched 106 times and rescued 32 lives.

Duet

Linton Hope was a designer of fast and beautiful boats. Not just deep water cruisers and racers; but International Canoes, the Broads One-Design, Thames Raters and, just before and during WW1, the hulls of the first flying boats. In 1912, a 50 ft gaff-rigged yawl was built by White Bros on the river Itchen to his design; oak frames, teak planking and American rock elm below the waterline. She was named **Gaviota** (Spanish for sea-gull).

In the winter of 1930/31 the arctic explorer August Courtauld, virtually buried alive under snow in Greenland, kept himself together by dreaming about his ideal boat. He was part of an expedition that was gathering meteorological data for a possible air route to North America via the Arctic, hence the need to take vital weather readings through the darkness of the Arctic winter. They established a weather station on the ice-cap but finding themselves short of rations went back to base while August volunteered to man it alone. He was there for five months, for the last six weeks of which he was actually trapped and buried in his tent under the snow with just a ventilator pipe for air and running out of food and fuel. Two plans occupied his thoughts; the first to marry his future wife Mollie and the second to design his ideal cruising yacht. He was eventually rescued and after his safe return to England, found his bride and also the yacht **Gaviota** which he renamed **Duet** in honour of his marriage.

Had she been a smack, perhaps she might have been named the August & Mollie (or even the A&M); but the evocative **Duet** (which can actually be a girl's name - Google reports it as the 19,747th most common girl's name in the USA) described so elegantly both the yacht which they loved and the sailing that they would do together.

Duet OYC 21st anniversary rally September 1981

photo by © Beken

They relished their cruising together; but the offshore races, mainly North Sea and Scandinavia, tended to be boys only. Quite a lot of these were wins, either line honours or on corrected time.

Cruises were in and around British waters; Denmark, Sweden, Norway and a bit into the Baltic; several times to Brittany; once to the Med. In October 1949 **Duet** set out for the West Indies, but was prevented from getting there by heavy weather. "They set out from Teignmouth and encountered some heavy weather with strong head winds in the Bay, reaching Corunna after eight days. After the battering they received various repairs were necessary…..

"A week later they set out again and were met by even worse weather. The staysail split from luff to leach and for several days they either lay hove to or tried to get to windward under the trysail. In these conditions progress was extremely slow and it was clear that the crew would

Duet America's Cup Jubilee August 2001
photo by © Beken

be running out of time: my father had promised them that they would be home by Christmas. If they were to carry on he would be left single-handed after reaching the West Indies, so he decided to put the helm up and head for home. Now they were running with a big following sea. It was blowing a full gale which continued to increase; they handed the trysail and paid out warps astern. Later the tiny "spitfire" jib had to come in too and they ran under bare poles; even with nothing set she was doing six knots. The glass was falling fast. Suddenly they were overwhelmed by a huge sea breaking aboard and my father was swept out of the cockpit, mercifully being kept from going overboard by the guard rails. She broached to and he let her lie with the helm lashed down. The mizzen boom was broken and down below the

batteries and cabin table carried away. Seas kept breaking aboard and they had to keep pumping the bilges continually. They put out oil bags, got out the heavy towing warp, secured it to the mast and paid it out over the bow. With a small hatch cover lashed in the mizzen rigging she then rode more easily and took no more water aboard.

"The glass, after reaching the lowest my father had ever seen, started to rise and the wind blew harder than ever. The next day the storm died down and they could once more set their course for home. Some days later the Start was sighted from the masthead. It was a Sunday and they held a thanksgiving service on deck." Christopher Courtauld

From 1960 to 1994 she was on loan to the Ocean Youth Club (which became the Ocean Youth Trust) and is now on loan to the Cirdan Sailing Trust. In this half century she has taken some 8,000 young people to sea and, for certain, changed for the better the lives of many of them.

She has continued to take part with some success in races, including Tall Ships Races, evoking appreciation and admiration wherever she goes. One of the nicest tributes came from the pen of WM Nixon, writing in *Yachting Monthly* in 1981, referring to her participation in the 1975 Jubilee Fastnet Race: "She was a clear line honours winner in the gaff rigged section… She would also be a clear winner were there a competition for the yacht which has contributed most to sailing in this century. In her own quiet way, **Duet** has had an unrivalled career, and will thoroughly deserve all the honours which come her way this month at the OYC birthday party." A further thirty years on and this is still true.

Rosabelle and Elfreda

(and Rosabelle and Rosabelle)

Theodore Pim was a clearly successful stockbroker for whom, in 1875, John Harvey of Wivenhoe built the first **Rosabelle**, a 76 foot square stern yawl. Ten years later he sold her and had built, in the same yard (but by this time Harvey was no longer in business and the yard was owned by Joseph Edwin Wilkins) the **Elfreda**, also a yawl but 104 feet in length. Wilkins' fourth daughter was born in 1886 and named Elfreda; but we can only guess as to whether she was named for the yacht or vice versa. Mr Pim was a prominent member of a well-known Anglo-Irish family; but nowhere in their extensive genealogical archives can the names Elfreda or Rosabelle be found. Who was Rosabelle?

Joseph Wilkins gave up his yard in 1888 and became first naval architect to Cox and King and designer of many of the firm's best known steam yachts, including **Gunilda**, **Venetia** and Mr Pim's second **Rosabelle**, which was built in 1897 by Ramage and Ferguson in Leith.

Rosabelle II   *Nottage Maritime Institute*

She was 147 feet long and had the beautiful clipper bow, fine figure-head, raked single funnel and two masts, which epitomised the elegance in design as sail gave way to steam. The era of these steam yachts - these salt water palaces - began in 1830 and lasted for just over a century. They could set 10,000 to 20,000 square feet of sail; but one wonders how often they did.

Rosabelle III   *Nottage Maritime Institute*

A third **Rosabelle** was built for Mr Pim in 1901, again designed by Wilkins and built by Ramage; she was 192 feet long. **Rosabelle III** served with the Royal Navy in both World Wars and was sunk by a German submarine in 1941.

Theodore Pim is remembered fondly in Wivenhoe, the village that built two of his four vessels, designed all four and provided their Captains, crew and winter quarters in mud berths. Rosabelle Avenue keeps their memory alive, as do Anglesea (sic) Road and Paget Road for Wivenhoe's great yachting patrons of the previous century.

Gunilda
from top to bottom

Sitting on the bottom of Lake Superior in 268 feet of water is the wreck of the Steam Yacht **Gunilda**. She is one of Canada's (if not the world's) best diving wrecks and her location is often referred to by divers as the G Spot. Built at Leith in 1897 her third owner was a New York oil magnate William Harkness, who, in 1911, was on an extended cruise of the Great Lakes. Declining, against his Captain's advice, to pay the fee of a pilot to navigate the Schreiber Channel, the **Gunilda** ran on to McGarvey's Shoal, which rises from 280 feet to 3 feet below the surface. All aboard were rescued; but as a tug towed her off (again against the advice of her Captain) she sank to the bottom. The Cousteau Society once visited the wreck of the **Gunilda** and claimed it was the most well-preserved (due to the intensely cold fresh water) and prestigious shipwreck in the world.

These astonishing photographs taken in 2000 by Dan Lindsay of Sea-View Diving (www.sea-viewsearch.com) show her gold leafing still marvellously preserved.

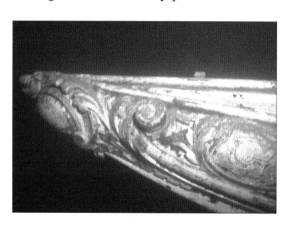

We do not know for whom she was named; but Gunilda or Gunhilda means battle maid in Norse. The Slavic Princess Gunhilda, daughter of King Mieszko I of Poland married King Sweyn Forkbeard and in about 994 they had a son who was to become the ruler of an empire which, at its height, included England, Denmark, Norway and part of Sweden: Canute the Great. Canute's daughter, also Gunhilda, married King Henry III of Germany, later Holy Roman Emperor.

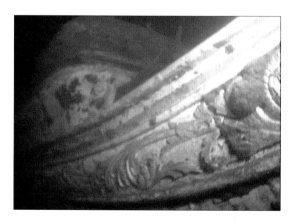

...in 268 feet of water...

Venetia

Gunilda's second owner was F W Sykes of Huddersfield (a manufacturer of card clothing - carding, ie combing / teasing wool - and fine wire); but in 1903, having sold her to Mr Harkness, he decided to ask the same designers and yard to build him a broadly similar but bigger vessel, the **Venetia I**, 272 feet overall and 595 tons gross (Gunilda was 195 feet overall and 385 gross tonnage). Launched in 1904, she cruised to the Dardanelles (fitted with bow chaser guns just in case!) and was then sold to an American, who, presumably, made an offer that Mr Sykes could not refuse. Straight away Cox and Kings were asked to design a very similar, but slightly smaller vessel, **Venetia II**, again built at Leith.

Whilst in Mr Sykes' ownership, both **Gunilda** and **Venetia II** were captained and crewed from Wivenhoe and laid up there in the winter. The boats carried by a steam yacht such as the **Venetia** would have been a rowing dinghy, a sailing cutter, a lifeboat and a rowing gig. The gig was the fastest of these and was used principally by the owner, his family and guests and for racing the gigs of other yachts. The gig of **Venetia II** was built by James Husk & Son Ltd of Wivenhoe in 1905.

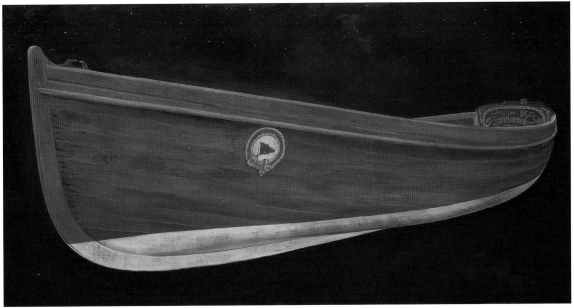

Venetia's gig   *painted by James Dodds*

She has been described by Mr Husk's granddaughter as "the most beautiful boat that I have ever seen", and she has seen a great many boats! By the time she was ninety (the gig not the granddaughter), she was in a pretty sorry state; but after a two years refit in Jim Spencer's yard in Brightlingsea, she competed in five Great River Races (22 miles from Ham to Greenwich), several times winning the Cup for the finest Historic Vessel, before retiring to a museum on the Upper Thames. She can be seen overleaf, as a centenarian, taking part in the 2005 race with a crew that boasted between them two world championship golds, one Olympic silver, nine Henley wins, four Boat Race victories (all for Cambridge) and two Head of the River wins.

"the most beautiful boat that I have ever seen"

Venetia's gig. Great River Race 2005 *photo by the author*

Once again we do not know for whom FW Sykes named **Venetia**. His great grandson said that he knew of no Venetia in the family and added (not terribly helpfully!) that two of his mill engines were named after his daughters, one of whom, Winifred, is seen here standing in front of **Venetia's** engine.

Winifred Sykes *photo James Walker*

Lucy

The 46 foot steel yawl **Lucy** was built in 1965 at the Scheepswerf Kok in Vinkeveen, Holland. Many of its yachts, including **Lucy**, were designed by Henk Tingen and with their exceptionally beautiful lines were excellent sea-boats; unsurprisingly, perhaps, as Henk Tingen also designed for Royal Huisman, which, founded in 1884 and granted a Royal Warrant on its centenary, still builds some of the most elegant yachts in the world.

Much of her early life was spent around Rhode Island, where she sank. Rescued, rebuilt and restored, **Lucy** is back where she belongs - one of the nicest looking girls afloat.

Lucy   *photo by Den Phillips*

Now owned by the best photographer of boats on our coast (perhaps all coasts), the temptation to sit in a dinghy all day long with a camera while your husband sails round you must be almost irresistible!

Den at the helm of **Lucy**   *photo by Den Phillips*
                                                    (well, by her camera anyway)

The Royal Burnham One Design

White Rose, Lavender Lady, Belinda, **Annette, Vaurnine, Jade, Beryl, Simonetta, Sapphire, Muriel, Ariel, Coral, Rae and Amanda..........**

...............one and all the very nicest-looking-girls-afloat; but then, of course, they are a one-design. And there is a lady alive today who was named by her parents for their RBOD.

Annette   *by Den Phillips*

Maybe this is a commendable Burnham-inspired habit, for **Mehalah's** owners, whom we met earlier in this book, have a daughter named for their previous boat **Lora**; like the RBODs a Burnham-built vessel.

Lora was built in 1911 by William King & Sons at Burnham-on-Crouch to the design of J Pain Clark, a barrister in Gray's Inn. Between the wars she raced out of Burnham very successfully in Thames Estuary and North Sea races. In 1900 Pain Clark had designed a cruising canoe and **Lora's** design owed much to this earlier boat and Pain Clark's belief that best results were achieved with the greatest wetted length and the least weight and windage. She was 30 feet long, 24 feet on the water-line, had low free-board and a canoe stern; a beautiful design for smooth water and light winds, leaving not a vestige of wake. Although wet in rough waters, she was immensely sea-worthy and in 1959 (now Bermudan rigged) she took part in the Fastnet Race. But **Lora's** greatest triumph was winning the RORC North Sea Race from Harwich to the Hook of Holland in 1957; First in Class 3 and First Overall. To win your first ever RORC race at the advanced age of 46 is something pretty special. Pain Clark is thought to have designed no more than 15 yachts, of which **Lora** was probably the best known because of her speed, plus the Royal Corinthian One Design Class (all named after birds), again built by William King at Burnham. These raced at Burnham until replaced by a new design in 1931.

But we must return to the Royal Burnham One Design.

During the years 1930 to 1935 the ex 24 ft. Class, all by then 30 to 40 years old, and racing on an arbitrary handicap system, was clearly disintegrating and it was clear that another class must be found. The final choice was between the X One Design Class, well established on the South Coast, and a new design by Norman Dallimore (Dalli), himself a member of the Club.

Dalli's design was chosen and building began immediately at William King & Sons. By the spring of 1933 nine boats had been built. Members of the Colne Yacht Club also built to the design at Douglas Stone & Son in Brightlingsea and named their boats for semi-precious stones: **Jade, Onyx, Quartz** etc.

Bermudan sloops 20 ft. long overall, about 17 ft. on the waterline and with a transom stern, they are fairly heavy boats with an iron ballast keel on a long fin. By 1939 twenty-three had been built to the rule and the present fleet of nine (with a handful more ready to go into the water or awaiting restoration) still has a full summer's racing programme. At the end of June each year the RBODs race off-shore to Brightlingsea and back the following day, after a fine evening's entertainment at the Colne Yacht Club. The races are timed to take advantage of the tide in the Ray Sand Channel. It's a long way round the Buxey and through the Wallet Spitway.

The Brightlingsea One Design

Jean, Mavis, Maida, Sybil, Mildred (Edwina), Bidi, Ann, Hilda, Lynette, Aina, Nan, Krystina, Brunette, Sarah Louise, Sabrina, Janice and Greta ....

.... again they are all the very nicest-looking-girls-afloat, and they, too, are a one-design.

At the AGM of the Brightlingsea Sailing Club in March 1927, the late Robbie Stone, son of Douglas Stone, trading as Douglas Stone and Son (later to be part of the amalgamated James and Stone), produced the plans of an 18 foot centre-board dinghy. The BOD was born. They are clinker-built, originally planked in elm, but later in mahogany. **Jean** was the first - Sail no. C1 - owned for her first few years by Robbie Stone himself. The following year Peter Courtauld, the Commodore, bought C3, and his Aunt Min, Miss K.M. Courtauld, C2, **Mavis**.

THE YACHTSMAN AND MOTOR BOATING July 2nd 1932
reported the **First Ladies' Race at Brightlingsea**

"Miss K. Poole delighted at winning a Second Prize in **Jumbo Too**, Jack Maltby's new B.O.D.C. The crew R. Stone and Tom Bishop aft." *photo thought to be by Douglas Went - Mersea Museum*

The last wooden boat was built in 1989 by Malcolm Goodwin who, in 2004, relaunched **Jean** after a ten year restoration. In 2007 the first GRP BOD, **Greta**, was built by John Mullins. There have been 41 built (38 wood and 3 GRP); 21 are still sailing and 7 are currently being restored.

One of the most coveted cups for which the class races is the Vergemere Trophy. The Steam Yacht **Vergemere** belonged to Betty Carstairs, the American heiress to a Standard Oil fortune who, in 1931, was the first lady commodore of the Colne Yacht Club. She had a fleet of yachts including the three-masted schooner **Sonia** of 450 tons, an eight metre **Baby Sonia** and the **Vergemere** of 114 tons.

Mate of the big **Sonia** and skipper of **Baby Sonia** was Jack Francis, who, aged 11 in 1914, ran away from home because his father, Joseph, would not take him to sea with him in his 30ft fishing boat, the **Ant**. He walked to London ("by following the telegraph poles"), got to the River where the police caught him and returned him to Brightlingsea, where his father gave him a "good leathering"; but then relented and took him to sea. Jack became foreman of the Colne Fishery Company and then, in 1961, Colchester Oyster Fisheries. Another baby Sonia, his daughter, was born in 1931.

"A study of the B.O.D.C. at the start of the second round. **Cormorant** (4) sailed by Miss Hoborn leads, **Mavis** (2) sailed by Miss K.M. Courtauld won, with **Jumbo Too** (6) second."

photo thought to be by Douglas Went - Mersea Museum

Brightlingsea One Designs

photo by Den Phillips

Film Stars

Wr began with one film star, the little winklebrig **Joy**. We end with ten film stars, all BODs.

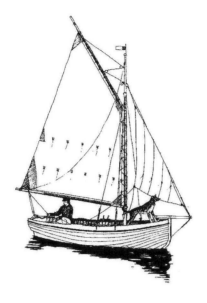

In the summer of 1986 a film was made for American TV, *The Ted Kennedy Jr. Story*, about Senator Edward Kennedy's (Craig T. Nelson) son Ted (Kimber Shoop) who had, at the age of 12, lost a leg to a rare form of cancer. Apparently Cape Cod had changed somewhat in the thirteen years since the events portrayed in the film had taken place and by 1986 Brightlingsea and its boats were more like the Cape Cod of 1973 than Cape Cod itself was. So Brightlingsea hard and the Colne became a film set for two days, with ten BODs playing their part as good old Essex troupers, to portray the Kennedy family at play back home, just as the Walton Backwaters had for the filming of *The Snow Goose*; Fritha saying farewell to Philip Rhayader as he set off for Dunkirk.

THE END

Epilogue

Nowadays it would be easy to conclude that, apart from the enormous container ships and ferries coming out of Harwich harbour or smaller tankers and gravel barges going up and down the Thames, this coast is merely a small boat sailor's play-ground. But scratch the surface of the waterfront villages and towns and you will find underneath an unbelievable richness. The families of those whose living was the harsh reality of the North Sea in all its moods are still there, guardians of the history, much of it well documented and certainly well remembered. If that were not the case, I could not have taken my readers on the butterfly journey which this story has proved to be. Thank you to all those who have helped me mine that rich ore, especially………..

………. John Collins, archivist of Nottage Maritime Institute, and James Dodds for their help and encouragement in so many ways (not least for allowing me to quote from their recent book, River Colne Shipbuilders); Tony Millatt, of Mersea Museum, for helping me so much with pictures in their collection, particularly those taken by Frank Thompson and Douglas Went and those from the John Leather collection; Janet Harker, who drew the snow goose and her winklebrig Joy; Neil Jones, archivist of Trinity House for the picture of Patricia; Richard Basey and Margaret Cormack, Vice-Commodore and Hon. Secretary of the Association of Dunkirk Little Ships, for allowing me to quote so much from their web site; David Page of Navy Photos (Galatea); Kathy Knight, for letting me quote from Hervey Benham; June Fisher, whose late husband's paintings hang above my desk; Dan Lindsay of Sea-View Diving who let me use his astonishing underwater pictures of Gunilda; Den Phillips, for so many of her photographs and whose patience was inexhaustible; Richard Titchener for his unerring advice on where I could find so much that I needed; Michael Feather for giving me so much about Letitia; Douglas McCarthy, National Maritime Museum, for the picture of the Pearl (PU6502); Stephen Gregor for his pictures of the bronze sculpture of Boadicea; Paul Winter for his pictures of Maria; Peter Mumford of Beken for the pictures of Duet; David Truzzi-Franconi and Caroline Spencer for the pictures of Jim; Leslie Head who helped so much with all things to do with Burnham; Andrew Pool and the Royal Cornwall YC for the photograph of The King's racing flag; Rupert Marks, James Lawrence, Christopher Kerrison, Guy Taplin, David Cole, Gay Edwards, Reuben Frost, George Courtauld, George Paul, Richard Smith and, above all, Christopher Courtauld who, without complaint, proof read and, with his great wisdom, contributed to draft after draft. Finally I would like to thank Essex Heritage Trust for its generous contribution to printing costs. Thank you all.

David Starling 2011

Oystercatcher
by Guy Taplin

Index